The Tree Poets

The Tree Poets

A Life of Sand

Annie Cowell

Kerry Darbishire

Patricia M Osborne

First published 2025 by The Hedgehog Poetry Press

Published in the UK by
The Hedgehog Poetry Press
5, Coppack House
Churchill Avenue
Clevedon
BS21 6QW

www.hedgehogpress.co.uk

ISBN: 978-1-913499-89-1

Copyright © Mark Davidson 2025

The right of Mark Davidson to be identified as the editor of this work has been asserted in accordance with the Copyright, Designs and Patents Act 1988. All rights for individual works retained by the respective author.

All rights reserved. No part of this publication may be reproduced, stored in or introduced into a retrieval system, or transmitted in any form, or by any means (electronic, mechanical, photocopying, recording or otherwise) without prior written permissions of the publisher. Any person who does any unauthorised act in relation to this publication may be liable for criminal prosecution and civil claims for damages,

9 8 7 6 5 4 3 2 1

A CIP Catalogue record for this book is available from the British Library.

Annie Cowell 7

    How I've outlived a Queen 9
    Sunday Lunch 10
    The robin prefers a suet ball......................................11
    I am Carolina Reaper 12
    A grandma tree 13

Kerry Darbishire 15

    The Water Between my Father and Me 16
    In the Distance 18
    Heysham...19
    Iona in May 20
    You Ask Me Why I Stay..21

Patricia M Osborne 23

    Little Green Suit 25
    Mini Mum 26
    Easter Holiday:1966..27
    One became Two..28
    Wishing Stone 29

ANNIE COWELL

HOW I'VE OUTLIVED A QUEEN

advice from my 98 year old father - in - law

Live simply.
Eat plain food; porridge made with water,
banana sandwiches, soup (tinned is fine);
leave that last slice of cake for someone else.
Read books borrowed from the library
or bought for pennies in a charity shop,
return them when you're finished.
Walk every day, come rain or shine;
keep an eye on the sky so you know
when to hang out your washing
or if you'll need a brolly.
Talk to strangers in queues.
Listen.
Listen to the sea and the chatter of sparrows;
they're reliable and the gossip is harmless.
Try and avoid the news; it will only make you cry.
Kiss and make up, grudges are malignant
Sing.
Dance.
Laugh.
Feed the birds in the garden
and chase the cat when it comes hunting
the blackbird who lives under the bush.
Leave the weeds for the bees
and don't dust away cobwebs. Spiders
are good company in the cold winter months.
Place flowers on the graves of loved ones,
and tell their stories to your children.
Good manners cost nothing
so always
say thank you.

SUNDAY LUNCH

rituals began on Saturday with a bag
of veg dad brought from his allotment. It was
a lucky dip of corkscrew carrots, spuds
like hearts and asteroids, huge heads of cabbage.
Before bed mam would place dried peas, hard as
ball bearings, in a cold bath to soak; by Sunday
morning, when Karen Carpenter's vinyl voice
crooned gently from the living room,
they would've relaxed a little, be ready
for a slow stew to green mush.
With dad dispatched to the workies
mam could work her alchemy. It was a
familiar mystery; each week she charmed
those crooked veg into elixir. By the time
dad returned brimming with beer and
baccy the house was awash with scents
of pork and gravy.
Together at the table we tucked into
plates piled high, a giant
Yorkshire Pudding like a clown's hat
perched on top. We ate till we could barely
move then begged like Oliver Twist
for more. Dad stole my pork; a secret
gift that silenced my meaty demons.
There was magic in those meals.
Later, when life had moved us on to
Sunday lunches far away, the echo of dad's
'that was beautiful, pet' as he squeezed mam's hand
 pushed back his chair and left the table
would remind us of those golden days.

THE ROBIN PREFERS A SUET BALL.

For years dad sat in his chair
with a pile of finger nails on the window ledge
beside him, with which he
picked his teeth. Often,
there was a banana under his armpit,
tucked inside his shirt
my sister warned me about the banana
'Don't mention it,'she said.
Dad watched the garden from his chair.
It was better than watching TV, which made him cry.
The bird table gave him an endless loop of
sparrows, blue - tits and the robin.
He studied the robin through tunnel vision -
remembered that it preferred a suet ball to a raisin
when he couldn't even remember the day
Knew its song
and would turn his face to the glass at its sound
'My mate,' he would say
And smile.

I AM CAROLINA REAPER

I am a sky of nimbostratus, sagging
with rain, plumes
of cumulonimbus rising, sparks

I am a headless chicken,
body flapping in circles
as my eyes watch, separate

I am a crinkled Carolina Reaper;
a red - faced stop light

I am lady Macbeth, wish fulfilled,
unsexed
a half burnt candle

Murderous as a cornered cat, feral.
A mole, in a hole.

I am a lady bird; my house is on fire,
my children are gone.

I am a page full of smudges
and mistakes. Waiting
to be re - written.

A GRANDMA TREE

When the swallows come shrieking news of spring
I will hold your hand
and we'll toddle to the garden together.
We will dig a hole, feel
the soil between our fingers
as we plant a
tree. Lemon perhaps, or cypress. Together we will
water it, tend it, watch it grow In time we will
spread a rug
sit in the green shade
watch for bees bouncing in
the lavender, lizards
scuttling to the shadows.
We will kick up our heels in bougainvillea petals
and flicker like motes in the sun.

KERRY DARBISHIRE

THE WATER BETWEEN MY FATHER AND ME

'Your skin   craters   curious   deep
                                    mine   soft as the moon's halo

Your eyes   tides hauling sunsets across the bay
                                    mine   mornings clear as birdsong

Your mouth   shells on the shore
                                    mine   wings fluttering a meadow

Your nose   knowing a lamb stew ready
                        mine   not knowing   tobacco   old spice   gin

Your ears   stalactites in the dark
                                    mine   feathers on a path

Your hands   warm as a hearth
                                    mine   bundled into yours

Your feet   rivered boulders
                                    mine   pushing upstream

Your hair   uniform-short   rain-smooth
                    mine   longing for plaits and ribbons to tap my back

Your throat   a westerly
                                    mine   an easterly

Your breath   owls in the ghyll
                                    mine   the weave of a wren's nest

Your bones   an oak marking a curve in the river
                                    mine   a sapling willow

Your blood   the estuary
                                    mine   a spring

Your mind   a riverbed after a storm
            mine   a stream of sticklebacks   frogspawn   marigolds

Your heart   rock ledges in mist
                                    mine   deer tracks in snow

Your love   a map of stars   mine   the compass you gave me

IN THE DISTANCE

My father lifts plates down from the rack,
    pulls knives and forks from a crumb-held drawer
whistling and humming
                      Red Sails in the Sunset.
In a room of flock walls and uncut moquette
    I'm popping plastic beads together
making a necklace for him
                    listening
to the softness of slippers like boats
    crossing calm lakes of lino' in a kitchen
of spitting lard   a smoking pan
                      the promise
of fritters   on our table wiped to a Formica sheen.
    He's calling   *Poppet* – the name he gave me
the full sail of it   the ghost of a smell
                                in the air

HEYSHAM

July-blue sky and the school trip
    we saved for all year.
The Brown's coach charged with
        I do like to be beside the seaside,
Stewart on the back seat stuffing his pale-
    as-a-paper-bag face with a pie. Hazel slapping
on lipstick the colour of Morecambe rock and by ten o'clock
    our grease-proofed sandwiches eaten or squashed.
Shrimp and vinegar air pulled us high as kings and queens
    along the prom and by the afternoon we flagged
in sand-stuck hours, a veiled horizon, screams
    from the dipper, our hands stinging and sore
in waves circling the finest castles we ruled for a day.

IONA IN MAY

Following the old ways
in they fly: corncrakes, swifts
and swallows wing-heavy
with cloud, salt and storm
to summer nesting ground.

Generations of pilgrims return
to this sacred island, like the visitors
I see now swarming off the ferry,
bowed down, pulling suitcases, burdens
too heavy.

in a whisper of waves, Iona opens
her arms smooth as waves over pebbles
and under an ever-changing sky,
answers their prayers, sets them free,
light as fledglings.

YOU ASK ME WHY I STAY

after Ocean Voung

To remember our first winter together.

For wild geese returning north and south in waves of song.

To watch morning sun pour itself down the fell like honey on bread.

To hear you strike a match in the blackened hearth.

For the first two notes of a cuckoo in May.

For a glass of fell water. Moon-soaked fields. Your breath upon the frosty air.

To know the next thing.

To see three pheasants roosting in the pine tree outside my window.

For your touch lovely as a ripe apple I didn't eat straight away.

To watch a goldcrest caper on stems of clematis.

Because my children will always want to ask me something.

To watch your gift of bluebells spread like a wide fallen sky.

For the air through my bedroom window carrying night sound.

For rain in all her moods.

For your river of words always knowing which way to go.

To say the things I haven't learned yet.

PATRICIA M OSBORNE

LITTLE GREEN SUIT

I cried at bath time, not wanting to go to bed, but Mum
perched me on the counter, told me I was going out instead.

She dressed me in a little green suit, two straps held the green-fleck
pleated skirt in place. I slipped my arms into the matching jacket.
Mum said I looked delightful making me beam inside.

Dad took me on a train, what fun that was, but my little legs ached
from traipsing the long avenue with a tall wall all down one side.

We reached a huge forecourt with red-paved tiles,
I rang the bell, white-haired Nanna opened the door,
greeted us with a smile – I jumped up and down.

Her wooden bricks were brilliant to play with but I hated
using the stone potty at night-time when I needed a wee.

Grandad picked up Mum and I from our top flat,
drove us in his white van to Liverpool
to grey-haired granny's who owned a shop.

I squeezed her tight. She gave us Cherry B,
only a drop for me but Grandad drank
too much so couldn't drive us back home.

Mum made a bed on the couch, we slept snug
side by side on pillows in plastic bags
with a big, soft blanket keeping us warm.

I cried when I grew taller and my little green suit
became too small. I hid in my room cos night-time
escapades stopped, but I clapped my hands high

when my baby brother was born and Nanna, Grandad
and Granny came to visit us all in our brand-new house.

MINI MUM

Mum leans over the mesh fireguard
to look in the mirror.

Her lurex frock clings to her teeny waist,
glittery fabric brushes gold high-heel shoes.

She unclips foam curlers,
bouncy chestnut waves
fall one by one
and hug her dress.

After dabbing perfume behind her ears,
Mum unravels my palm and pats
a drop on my wrist.

She traces rose-red lipstick around her mouth,
blots a tissue on her plump lips, bends down
to me, dabs my lips sticky – lifts me up to see.

EASTER HOLIDAY:1966

Nanna showered me with broken chocolate eggs
from Great Aunty Zena's shop and told me to eat
them all up before my holiday came to an end.

Those Magnificent Men in their Flying Machines,
raced in the air, monochrome fun on a huge
Cinerama screen made me laugh and clap.

At Chester Zoo, giraffes bent long necks, my neck
hurt from looking up at them. Elephants sucked water
through trunks, squirted it into their mouths,

monkeys did acrobatics on bars in the cage,
giant polar bears growled making me shake.

Nanna lifted me on her lap. 'Teresa,
will you stay here forever to keep me company?'

I shook my head. 'I love you, Nanna, but miss
my sisters, miss my mum and miss my home.'

Dad packed my bag in the boot of the Ford Zephyr.
Nanna cried. 'Teresa, come back again soon.'

At bedtime I snuggled up with my sister, Mum read
a story, kissed us good night, and said, 'Teresa,
it's lovely to have you back – I missed you.'

ONE BECAME TWO

for my sister, Heather
(9th May 1956 – 14th July 2009)

First there was one and then one became two,
the day you arrived was Bobbsey for me.
From that day on we were inseparable,
two girls dressed the same, as twins like to be.
We'd sing to vinyl forty-fives and step
sideways in routine, both arms wide up high,
drink tea and trick *Pisha Pashya* with decks
of cards or flirt with boys making them shy.

As we grew taller and ripened in years,
the time came to go our separate ways,
you soared over wild waves high in the air,
to fulfil your dream, gone were jester days.
Malignancy struck, you fought a fierce war,
battled and lost, leaving one – as before.

WISHING STONE

I pick up a pale grey rock
from the pebbled shore,
inspect its white quartz belt.

Using my finger, I trace
the chalky unbroken line
and close my eyes.

I throw the stone far out to sea
and watch the waves swallow
my wish, swimming it away.